Beauty of
Utah

Beauty of

Utah

Text: Paul M. Lewis

Concept & Design: Robert D. Shangle

First Printing January, 1989
Published by LTA Publishing Company
1425 S.E. 18th Avenue, Portland, Oregon 97214
Robert D. Shangle, Publisher

"Learn about America in a beautiful way."

Library of Congress Cataloging-in-Publication Data
Beauty of Utah
/concept & design, Robert D. Shangle; text, Paul M. Lewis.
      p.   cm.
ISBN 0-917630-68-8; $19.95. — ISBN 0-917630-67-X (pbk.); $9.95
    1. Utah — Description and travel — 1981 — Views. I. Shangle,
Robert D. II. Lewis, Paul M.
F827.B43   1989
917.92'0433 — dc19   88-37209
                                   CIP

Copyright © 1989 by LTA Publishing Company
Printed in Hong Kong by Beauty of the Americas Printing Company
Offices: Seattle, Washington; Portland, Oregon; Hong Kong

Contents

Introduction

What is a Utahan? A few centuries back it was, rather exclusively, a member of the Ute tribe, when the location of Utah was one of the world's best-kept secrets. Later the Mormons settled in west of the Wasatch and built a thriving agricultural economy and a strong church. Since then, of course, a lot of people of varied origins have moved into Utah.

Most of the people reside in Salt Lake City and its sister communities to the north and south along the western Wasatch ramparts. This leaves very few in eastern and southern Utah to meddle with the scenery. And that's a particularly fortunate circumstance in the case of Utah, where nature's timeless energies have wrought a landscape uniquely susceptible to injury. Restless, ambitious mankind has a well-known talent for altering the environment he lives in. More often than not, the terrain he changes suffers a depletion of natural values, esthetically and otherwise. In some cases, given enough time, these damaged places can repair themselves after we leave off "improving" them. Trees can grow, again, in a forest that has been ransacked for lumber. Rivers and streams will support fish populations, again, when they are no longer used as sewers. Land that has been over-grazed returns to health after it is given a rest.

But Utah's incredibly diverse and spectacular canyonlands are irreplaceable in human terms. The process of uplift and erosion that created them began before humankind was even in the planning stage. A soaring arch that stuns the senses by its simple grace, a crowd of rock pinnacles standing together as if waiting for a divine visitation, a slender rock bridge stretched over a stream bed or dry wash, even the fragile plant life that has achieved a shaky toe hold in the nooks and crannies of the canyons — all these marvelous bits of creation bear witness to the superhuman time scale of nature's work shedule.

Two big miracles have been necessary to make Utah's unique landscape possible. Both of them are still in process. The first miracle is the never-ending creative activity of great and small natural forces, building mountains and gouging canyons. The second miracle, less certain to last, is our growing awareness of our place in the chain of life. Maybe it will take another miracle to make this concept a permanent part of the human tradition.

P.M.L.

Zion and Bryce Canyons

Utah's most celebrated canyons are Zion and Bryce, in southwest Utah. The two areas are of especial interest to geologists because they reveal different, later periods of geologic history than does that super-spectacular, Grand Canyon. Zion was carved by the Virgin River out of the Markagunt Plateau, the river cutting about a half-mile into the plateau's sandstone. This erosional power of the river not only formed Zion Canyon, but in so doing revealed rock layers associated with middle periods of the earth's geologic history. Bryce Canyon is a still later event. Several miles northeast of Zion, it was fashioned out of the Paunsaugunt Plateau not by powerful rivers — like Zion and Grand canyons — but by the erosional action of seepage water, wind, rain, and freezing.

Zion's awesome vertical red rock walls are the result of a spectacular erosional process involving weaker rock at the base of the cliffs. The weaker rock is worn away more rapidly, undermining the rock above it. Great chunks of the overhanging rock split off into the river below, where they may have only a short rest. The powerful stream will soon carry them off, worrying the biggest rocks into smaller ones more amenable to eventual transportation. Some of Zion's monoliths rise a stunning 2,500 feet above the canyon floor, their red-rock faces setting off the lush green vegetation at the bottom. That hard-working river is a bit more impatient than the Colorado at getting on with the job. Its rate of fall at the canyon's north end, where the red walls press in closely on each other, is 90 feet for each mile; so the Virgin River rushes to meet the Colorado.

Zion's rock formations have been likened both to gothic and to classical architecture. Its monumental cathedrals and temples in the forms of cliffs and rock mesas have the clean, soaring lines of grecian art forms or Gothic masterpieces. The names given to the awesome rock monoliths strengthen this idea: the Great White Throne, a glittering white sandstone pile towering to an elevation of 6,744 feet; opposite, Angel's Landing, whose dull red rock is in contrast to the Throne; the Organ, a colossal projection of red rock mountains with vertical sides. West Temple is the highest point in the park, 7,795 feet in altitude (3,805 feet above the canyon floor). Its outsized proportions are not the only interesting feature of this structure: one side of its mass is like brilliant red-streaked marble, the background color being white, or cream.

Language is sadly over-matched when certain natural phenomena are being described. Zion's wonders impose silence. What can hyperbole do for the sight of the Watchman, across the canyon from the West Temple but more ornate and even more colorful? Its red rock is highlighted by green, orange, pink, and rust. A gargantuan cathedral of stone, it seems to be lighted by interior fires when the setting sun sets ablaze the brilliant hues of its face. The canyon and its park are filled with these awesome stone monuments, whose poetry is quite beyond language.

One's emotional responses to such grandeur are awe and reverence. Regardless of a person's religious fervor or lack of it, a prayerful attitude is simply imposed on the visitor, gazing in dumb admiration at what are surely the most superlative examples, on a grand scale, of natural art on the face of the earth.

Bryce is not really a canyon at all, having no river by which it stands at attention, as other canyons do. It is shaped like a horseshoe and gives an eerie impression of being peopled by larger-than-life statues of red rock. The "statues," or spires, carved in exquisite detail out of limestone and sandstone, have been compared to a silent city, or to candles on a pink and white birthday cake. The Paiute Indians believed the figures were once-living creatures turned to stone by evil spirits. The amphitheater cuts down about a thousand feet into the Paunsaugunt Plateau, revealing the primarily pink and white rock of the plateau. But almost an infinity of tints can be recognized by anyone who looks with discrimination at Bryce and its bizarre and beautiful forms. Nature may have no labels in mind when she chisels something out of stone, but man classifies things to make sense out of his surroundings and has neatly catalogued the canyon's rocky shapes as spires, temples, and domes. Flights of fancy are easy in a place such as Bryce.

The canyon is named for the 19th-century homesteader, Ebenezer Bryce, who, when asked to describe his namesake canyon, summoned up a rich, poetic image with, "Well, it's a hell of a place to lose a cow." Ebenezer may have lost quite a few cows if they wandered up into the canyon from his homestead to the adjacent valley. The tortured structures come in all sizes, the larger ones representing the ruins of caverns, cathedrals, dungeons, castles, and whatever — the smaller ones, soldiers and priests, queens and dowagers all scattered in great profusion throughout the "canyon," a crazy jumble of walls and ramparts, spires and pinnacles, gargoyles and gremlins.

One of the eternal fascinations of these canyonlands, especially in a gathering of rock fantasies like Bryce, is the power of light to alter tones, perspectives, and relationships. When the sky is studded with clouds, the alternating sunshine and shadow produces magical color changes in rock masses, varying from deep red to orange to brilliant yellow; light-colored formations glitter like bright gold when a cloud suddenly passes from the eye of the sun. And in the moonlight, the white spires seem to breathe a ghostly phosphorescence by contrast with the shadows that surround them in broken streaks of black. When a castle or a regiment or a rampart is suddenly brought into the spotlight of sunshine or moonlight it grows in size and importance for that brief time, then retreats into anonymity when the light passes from it. But perhaps the canyon is most beautiful in the early morning sun. The cream-colored limestone capitals turn a dazzling white, while farther into the canyon depths, deep roses, reds, coppers, and golds paint the jumbled forms with a warm radiance.

The visitor to Zion Canyon enters by the canyon floor and only takes to the rim if he feels the need for an overall view and has the ambition needed for the climb. Bryce Canyon, on the other hand, is viewed from the rim road, with trails to the floor that encourage more intimate visiting. The world of Bryce is equally enchanting close up.

Capitol Reef National Park

More than a quarter-of-a-million acres of the 11,000-foot Aquarius Plateau in southern Utah were given the protection of National Park status in 1971. Capitol Reef, formerly a national monument, now includes all of the previous protected area plus an additional corridor extending south to the Glen Canyon National Recreation Area. The reef is a sort of centerpiece to the Waterpocket Fold, a flexure or upthrust part of the earth's crust, about 100 miles long. Capitol Reef, itself, is essentially a ridge or cliff face about 20 miles long. Its spectacle combines the monumental grandeur of Zion with the bizarre fantasies of Bryce. Its colors are more than a match for the other two parks.

Wind and water are the sculptors of the sandstone wall that is Capitol Reef. Taking their time, these two artisans have chiseled huge arches and pinnacles, deep gorges and graceful bridges into the 1,000-foot-high barrier. Some of the brilliant sandstone layers have been weathered into rounded — "capitol" — domes. Waterpocket Fold, by the way, is named for the many natural "pockets" in the rock — some of them huge — that are full of water in the spring of the year. At one time the Indians were given credit for building the tanks, but now the big "bathtubs" are known to have been scooped out by waterfalls after the great fold was pushed up out of the earth. The whole area takes in some of the least-explored and wildest terrain left in the coterminous United States.

Petrified forests are another popular feature of Capitol Reef. About 25-square miles of the park are rich in petrified wood fragments, some very small and some huge. A tree in the Circle Cliffs area is, supposedly, 185 feet long and more than 12 feet through. The trees are measured as to length, because most of them have fallen. This seems to be a natural sequence of events in the process of petrification.

The park is also a treasure-house of human art (Indian variety). Petroglyphs were carved on the cliff walls by the Pueblo tribes, who also painted pictographs on the vertical rock barriers. The pictures represent domestic and wild animals and human figures. Examples of the wall carvings may be seen at the village of Fruita, on the Fremont River, at the western edge of the park. Artifacts of the basketmaker peoples are found here in abundance, and some of the Hopi granaries of adobe — those that have escaped the looters and souvenir-hunters — may still be seen. Fruita is an area of orchards, naturally, and the vivid green of the trees and the gardens is even brighter against the rich, warm colors of the tall cliffs that surround it. Just a few hundred yards from the town, but three miles by tortuous trail, is Broad Arch. The arch is massive — 133 feet from base to base — but looks quite tiny against a background of 2,000-foot cliffs.

Capitol Reef's most beautiful canyon is probably Grand Gorge. Down into the gorge are vivid red cliffs, a gigantic grotto 600 feet high with phenomenal acoustics, a 200-foot-high glistening rock wall of exceptional bands of color ranging from very dark to very bright, and a towering white monolith on a red rock base, resembling the Great White Throne of Zion National Park. Some parts of Grand Gorge are quite narrow — little more than slits — where the canyon walls are about 15 feet apart and rise steeply for about 600 feet.

Everywhere in Capitol Reef the colors are astounding for subtlety and range. Heroic walls of rock flaunt brilliant and warm reds, oranges, yellows, and creams; but softer shades of these tints are prominent, too, as well as purple, green, and blue, the latter two usually in pale and delicate tones. Capitol Gorge is no exception. Its walls and formations go from purple to red to cream and present a tremendous variety of forms. Pinnacles, cliffs, the monoliths are all brazen showoffs, appearing in countless shapes and rich colors. The gorge is one of those places in canyon country where peril is just around the bend of a rock wall. A part of it, called the Narrows, pinches in to about 18 feet, with walls that rise to 1,000 feet. Summer cloudbursts sometimes fill this narrow passage in a matter of minutes with raging torrents that carry all before them, including any unwise persons or animals who have stayed on the canyon floor too long.

Arches National Park

Just north of the town of Moab, and northwest of the Colorado River, is a part of the plateau that presents itself to the casual glance as a flat and lifeless desert, greenish-gray, punctuated here and there by red sandstone reefs. To the north rise the Book Cliffs of the Tavaputs Plateau. In the distant southeast, the LaSal Mountains form a white-crested backdrop. But there seems to be nothing much in between, if the view is from the highway that runs close by the park.

Reaching down below the level of the plain are remarkable canyons several hundred feet deep, steep-walled and difficult of access, except occasionally where side canyons split off from the main gorge. The remarkable part is not their depth. Most canyons in this canyon-crowded country have to go much deeper to get a small amount of attention. It's what is *in* these canyons that counts.

Arches' distinctive formations are wind-carved. The eternal wilds of the Colorado Plateau have been blowing for millions of years on relatively soft Entrada sandstone, pushed by pressures within the earth. The early forms emerged as "fins," slab-like structures that have been further eroding into natural arches and bridges. There are arches all over Utah's canyon country, but Arches National Park has the greatest concentration of them. Some 90 have been counted so far. And as Rainbow Bridge is to natural bridges, so Delicate Arch is to natural arches: the quintessential arch tops in the pantheon of natural arches. Its setting doesn't hurt, either. Delicate Arch rears its massive head far above the slick rock of the saucer-like "stage," where it stands in lonely splendor, a little below the canyon wall. Viewed with the LaSal Mountains as a backdrop, Delicate Arch is truly beautiful, changing its aspect with the changing light of day, dark and mysterious in the morning, blazing with golden glory at dusk.

The Devil's Garden section of Arches contains a bewildering assortment of wind-eroded forms. Here are most of the arches, along with great fins, giant amphitheaters, and grotesque monoliths. It must be explored on foot, especially the lower, Fiery Furnace part. Here the red canyon walls, red sandstone fins, and twisting trails conspire to create a maze that is difficult to get into and difficult to get out of. The Devil's Garden trail is several miles of fascination: traversing small canyons; passing many arches, including six major ones; and skirting many other weird sandstone shapes. Near where the trail takes off from the highway is Arch-in-the-Making, standing high on the canyon wall. This almost-arch has a huge cavity where rock was thrust out by expanding ice; now wind-blown sand is chipping away at the wall, which in some future millenium will be another arch. Farther along, about half a mile, is Pine Tree Arch, named for a rugged tree that grows under the center of the span. Then there's Hole-in-the-Wall, another half-mile away. It's high up the canyon face, like a giant eye commanding the tortuous and gothic landscape below. Near the trail's mid-point is the *piece de resistance*, Landscape Arch. Like a projectile trajectory, it swoops 118 feet above the rock floor and is 291 feet long. Landscape Arch is thought to be the longest natural span in the world. It is, assuredly, one of the most beautiful and graceful, only a few feet wide, with bands of black and salmon-colored stone. Beyond this point the trail grows steeper and the canyon narrower. Explorers in this portion will see still more arches through the stone corridors of the canyon, such as Double-O — double-deck windows — Navajo, and Partition arches.

Two other sections of the park are named The Windows and Courthouse Towers, each for obvious reasons. The Windows is a red sandstone cliff that rises out of the plateau for 300 to 400 feet. But it has holes in its head, so to speak. These are North Window and South Window, both about 65 feet high and 130 feet long. Because of their similarity, regular outlines and the imposing desert landscape seen through them, they are sometimes dubbed "Spectacles." The Windows Reef has some other noteworthy formations. A short trail hike from the Spectacles, via the Cove of Caves (an amphitheater where sounds reverberate), is Double Arch, two outsized stone arcs, salmon pink streaked with black.

Courthouse Towers lies below the desert in a canyon 400 feet deep. It begins just a few miles north of Moab, the park's "gateway" town. A scenic route through the Towers, called Park Avenue, brings to mind a stone-age Manhattan. A mile-long trail wanders between perfectly vertical walls of Entrada sandstone up to 300 feet high, a street of eroded "skyscrapers" without the noise and gasoline fumes. The trail passes the Three Gossips, giant rocks huddled together at the top of a 400-foot-high fin. And there is The Organ, a 700-foot-high fin, razor-thin at the summit. Trail's end is at the steep north wall of Courthouse Wash, where the "towers" that give the area its name are most apparent.

Grand and grandiose views, close-up and far away, are easily available at Arches. There are high points on the trails where the whole area spreads out before the eye. Adding beauty to beauty, the LaSal Mountains lend their gorgeous white raiment as background to several overlooks and arches. The world is indeed fortunate that enough people had the sense and foresight to set aside this unique part of the country, where nature has her way without human interference.

Bridal Veil Falls, Provo Canyon

Great Salt Lake

Monument Valley

North Window Arch in Arches National Park

Southwest Utah

Coral Pink Sand Dunes State Park

Temple Square, Salt Lake City

Mirror Lake in the Wasatch National Forest

Lake Powell

Landscape Arch, Arches National Monument

Mt. Timpanogos

Autumn in High Country North of Zion

Delicate Arch in Arches National Park

Flaming Gorge

Bryce Canyon National Park

High Country North of Zion National Park

Virgin River

State Capitol Building, Salt Lake City

Logan Canyon

Virgin River in Zion National Park

Trappers Lake near Buford

Angel's Landing, Zion National Park

Colorado River from Dead Horse Point

Sheep Creek Canyon near Flaming Gorge

Bear Lake, North of Logan

Ghost Town of Grafton, Southwest Utah

The Badlands West of Hanksville

Owachomo Natural Bridge, Natural Bridges National Monument

Navajo Twins

Red Canyon

Queen's Garden Trail in Bryce Canyon National Park

Badlands near site of Old Pariah

Steamboat Rock, Zion National Park

Capital Reef National Park

San Rafael Reef West of Green River

Capitol Reef National Park

Central Utah

Bryce Canyon National Park from Bryce Point

Colorado River in Canyonlands National Park

Cedar Breaks National Monument

Zion National Park

Fishlake National Forest

Ranch near Capital Reef National Park

High Country Autumn in Southwest Utah

Lake Powell near Hite

Southwest Utah Ranch

Church Rock, North of Monticello

Uintah Mountains

Canyonlands National Park

In 1964 part of a wild and forbidding expanse of southeast Utah became a national park. The chunk that received the protected status is called Canyonlands National Park, but the whole area, dominated by the Green, San Juan, and Colorado rivers, shares the freakish kind of terrain characteristic of the "slickrock" country. It has often been called a wasteland, a vast desert and sage plain where the weather is impossible for man or beast. Where the temperature ranges from plus 110°F. to minus 29°F., and the water supply — if any — is down in the canyons. Here cities fail to get built. This is, indeed, one of the wildest and least explored regions in the country. And its spectacular beauty derives mainly from the harsh climatic regime that makes it so inhospitable. Most of this high desert, or plateau, is a mile above sea level. Rainfall is less than ten inches a year, usually in the form of raging thunderstorms that carry away great layers of soil. Except where it is carved up by the three great rivers and their tributaries, this country is high and dry.

Canyonlands National Park is the centerpiece of this weird and mysterious land. Within its 257,640 acres are long stretches of the Green and Colorado rivers, each with its own spectacular and immensely varied reaches of canyon. Other canyons have been carved by the tributaries of these streams, but the ones on center stage are the work of the two major rivers. One of the very stylish gulches, indeed, occurs here, below the confluence of the Green and Colorado. This is Cataract Canyon. It extends south-westward to where Lake Powell begins, and, as the canyon's name implies, this is where the mighty river shows off its muscle. It flashes over its rocky bed in wild and exuberant fashion, hardly matched anywhere else within the Colorado's chasm.

The only "road" that goes all the way through this national park is the Colorado River, from the northeast to the southwest. The Colorado and the

Green are master streams, not only in the extent that they have carved up the Colorado Plateau, but in the authority which they exercise in forbidding all but the most minimal entry to the area by human intruders. For here, as in few other places on earth, the terrain seems to be not just indifferent to man's presumptive explorations, but actively hostile to any of his efforts to make it easier for a lot of people to visit the canyonlands. There are roads into the park, of course, but they are difficult affairs, reaching in from the north, east, and south. They are barely tolerated, cut off early in their careers by the sliced-up topography.

Of the many curiosities of canyon-carving that have intrigued visitors to this area of Utah, one example is found on the big river, itself. To see it from the best vantage point, one must sprout wings, or at least have the use of a helicopter. This is a spot just north of the Colorado-Green confluence, where the Colorado seems to lose its way and winds back upon itself in two immense loops. Someone named this formation The Loop. Two soaring mesas rise vertically more than 600 feet from the river, looking from the air like inverted pears placed next to each other. The larger one is about a mile long, the other about half that. Their clean, monumental structure and isolation between the meanders of the river give them a majesty hard to match even in this land where grandeur is commonplace.

Because Canyonlands National Park is so wild and rugged, unyielding in its intolerance of mechanized transportation, man finds himself on a more-or-less equal footing with the animals that live here.

That is the way to go — on foot. And in the process one stands a better chance of seeing some of the local residents, such as rabbits, reptiles, squirrels, kangaroo rats, and a great number of birds. Even bighorn sheep may be spotted, with luck. Foxes and coyotes live in canyon recesses, but they are good at hiding themselves. Four-wheel drive is possible in many areas, of course, as is horseback. But the surest way of getting to the remotest areas, over the up-and-down rocky topography, is with two strong legs attached to a pair of tough feet shod in hiking boots. And don't forget the water canteen.

One of the many canyons in the park that can only be explored on foot is

Elephant Canyon, at least along its upper reaches, about four miles in from the road in the southern part of Canyonlands. To get to that point the hiker goes through a maze of sandstone scuptures, whose culmination is the celebrated Druid Arch, at the head of the canyon, an incredible, knife-edged creation of red sandstone that stretches hundreds of feet into the clear desert air. Several miles to the east of Elephant Canyon is Salt Creek Canyon, which may be approached by four-wheel-drive or horse. Salt Creek is the home of the even more famous Angel Arch, the climax to the canyon's many noteworthy formations.

Canyonlands National Park is not known primarily for its arches, but it does have 25 such known formations. However, the place to observe arches, in all stages of building and destruction, is, of course, Arches National Park, which out-arches Canyonlands more than three to one.

The southeast area of the park is also known as Needles Country. It shares some erosional features with other parts of the park where weathering and jointing have created pinnacles, spires, balanced rocks, fins, and pillars. In The Needles, obviously, the predominant forms are the spires and similar forms that appear to be the last stages of the free-standing rock fins, carved out of rock masses by water and temperature extremes. Areas in or near the park, in addition to The Needles, where this kind of erosional action is especially evident, are the Fins, Monument Basin, and Standing Rocks, all locales west of The Needles. One of the most mysterious parts of the canyonlands, dubbed the Maze, is located in this general area west of the two rivers. Wild and almost inaccessible, this crazy jumble of canyons bespeaks nature's potential for inifinite complexity.

Finally, jutting into the northern park area is a large, plateau-like wedge that commands much of the space between the Green and Colorado rivers in this sector. The feature is called the Island in the Sky, and its cliff-like borders make it all the more distinctive from the surrounding terrain. It points a long, skinny finger south into the park, a finger ending in Grandview Point, an aptly named overlook commanding a sumptuous variety of views. The awesome canyons of the two big rivers stretch below; big Junction Butte rises in the south; the Standing Rocks country appears in the west; and the Needles formations can be seen in the distant southern sector of the park.

Certainly not all of the canyonland wonders have been gathered within the park's confines. Indeed, the hope is that even more of Southeast Utah will be added in the near future to one of the country's newer national parks. But the incredible kaleidoscope of forms and colors combined with immense stretches of open land and intricate canyons make Canyonlands Park a unique place on earth.

The North And The West

The harsh and rigorous climate, and the unusual geology that created the fantastic landscapes in the south, produced a different effect in the north. There is desert in the northwest, though it's not as interesting as the dry lands in the south. But on balance there are cities, people, agriculture, and snow-capped mountains, along with other scenic treats.

This part of Utah has its own interest. Even the barren monotony of the western Great Basin with its salt flats, wastelands, and dry valleys has a legitimate place on the landscape, if only to set off the more attention-getting areas. The Wasatch Range and the plateau land that continues from the range's end in Central Utah separate this nearly flat desert from the other worlds of Utah. One of those worlds is practically man-made. This is the narrow farming valley that lies between the Great Salt Lake and Utah Lake, on the west, and the Wasatch Range. A string of lush, green valleys about 150 miles long and 15 miles wide, it is known as the "Wasatch Front." Once desert land, like the country to the west, this strip has become fertile agricultural land. The Mormon settlers were the first to bring irrigation water from the mountains, and their Utah descendents have been doing it ever since.

Utah's biggest towns are in this north-central region. First comes Salt Lake City, then Ogden, Provo, and Logan. In an arid state, they and the other towns along the "Front" are green oases whose proximity to the abundant waters of the Wasatch makes them pleasant places to live. Their nearly mile-high elevation doesn't hurt, either. This part of the state is beautiful in a far different way from the southern portion. The two big mountain ranges create a big share of that beauty: the Wasatch, north-south, and the Uintas, east-west. Nestled within the broad shoulders of the Wasatch Range are some of the prettiest and most spectacular mountain valleys on the continent. Their proximity to the cities of the western slope has not greatly altered the stunning beauty of their wilderness forests — with some exceptions. The exceptions make up an important part of Utah's recreational industry, skiing. Probably the best skiing in the United States is possible on the dry powder snow of the Wasatch canyons. And some of the biggest and fanciest developments have been built to cater to the downhill racers. Three of the best known are Snowbird, Park City, and Alta (the oldest). There are about a dozen ski centers within an hour's drive of Salt Lake City, or even closer. So the best of two worlds is easily encompassed in one day — the diversions of a big city and the thrill of pine-scented mountain canyons.

Timpanogos Mountain — "Timp" for short — is a favorite of Utahans. High up on Timp's north slope is Timpanogos Cave National Monument. The mountain and the cave owe at least some of their popularity to being where the people are, on the Wasatch Front between Salt Lake City and Provo. American Fork Canyon, where the trail to the cave starts, has a rugged wilderness aspect that, surprisingly, has been little changed by its proximity to population centers. The rocky canyon with its steep walls is a spectacular gateway to the monument. The trail to the cave is a mile-long switchback pathway from where the scenery is more and more lavish as visitors ascend to the limestone cave 1,200 feet up the mountain. There are stunning views of the canyon, itself, and of the Utah Valley farming country beyond. The actual cave — really three connected caves — is believed to have been started about 50 million years ago along a fault line and enlarged through the eons of moving water. The water oozing through the limestone also created the formations that project from the cave's floor and ceiling.

The extreme northern corner of Utah can hold its own with the marvelous geology of the south. Ogden Canyon, between Ogden and Woodruff, is a fine example of this. There's no room at the bottom of this narrow gorge for anything but the Ogden River and the road. The canyon's walls present a picture of impenetrability, rising steeply several thousand feet. Where erosion has gained more of a hold, the sides retreat enough to make room for green park-like stretches along the river.

Another deep canyon of the north is Logan, whose walls rise for nearly a mile. At its highest, or deepest (depending on your perspective) points, it outdoes Grand Canyon, itself. The highest cliffs top out at 7,880 feet. At Logan Canyon's northeast end sits Bear Lake, half in Utah and half in Idaho, a large freshwater lake with white sandy beaches. Both the Ogden and Logan regions of the Wasatch Range are known for their excellent sports fishing and skiing. Camping is a popular activity in these precincts, too.

Some people like their mountains with fewer people under the trees — whether they be skiers, hunters, or just plain woods explorers. And northern Utah has the nation's largest east-west mountain range, the Uintas, which is just about unmatched for remoteness. The higher reaches of these northern Utah mountains make up a wilderness in the truest sense. This part is protected by Wilderness designation as the High Uintas Wilderness. Some 238,000 acres are included, straddling the crest of the range and including parts of the Wasatch and Ashley national forests. The proposal has been made to include even more land within the primitive area. Now that more and more outdoor-lovers have discovered the "remote" Uintas, some parts of them are showing signs of too much attention. The popularity of spectacular basin areas like Granddaddy Lakes, Four Lakes Basin, and Naturalist Basin — and others — have put them in some danger of injury from too many admirers.

Much of the less accessible Uinta country is above 10,000 feet in elevation. Kings Peak is the tallest in Utah at 13,528 feet, but the Uintas have twelve other giants over 13,000 feet. These high points are not "points" at all, literally. They do not stand erect like some other behemoths of the soaring Rockies. Their tops are roundshouldered — humpbacks, not spires. The Uintas are an upthrust range, geologists surmise, with an outer shell of softer, crumbly rock that has been subjected to glacial carving during various ice ages. Their variety of formations is remarkable. To offer a fanciful analogy, they look like the part of the southern canyonlands turned inside-out, or upside-down. Canyons are present here, too, along with huge rock outcroppings, stone amphitheaters, mesas, and monoliths.

The unique Uinta Range still has some mystery about it, just because some of its high recesses still pose a challenge to those who would penetrate its secrets. Although a major trail — Highline — goes the entire length of the range and has access trails leading from it to many parts of the range, the Uinta country is not yet all plotted and analyzed down to the last square inch. For the hiker, the climber, the backpacker — the person who is willing to test himself on a one-to-one basis with nature — this high-mountain sanctuary is a place whose attraction is second to none.

Northwestern and western Utah, as everybody knows, are great expanses of nearly nothing, interrupted by a lonely mountain here and there and, at its eastern edge, big, dead Great Salt Lake. Few things live in this region. The Lake, itself, occupies a depression in the Great Basin and has no outlet to the ocean. All of the mineral salts that flow into it remain there. They arrive there from Utah Lake to the south, via the Jordan River, and from Bear River on the north. Utah Lake is the largest freshwater lake in the state and has been used heavily for irrigation from the time the Mormons first chose Utah as "the place."

Extreme northern Utah boasts a natural feature that was created with man's active cooperation. This is the Bear River Migratory Bird Refuge on the river's delta, where it empties into Great Salt Lake. The area is between the Promontory Mountains and the Wasatch Range. The natural marshlands have been enhanced by dikes that spread out the water from the river, creating an ideal waterfowl habitat and nesting ground. In the fall, especially, ducks, geese, and other migratory birds hold great fly-ins. Established by Congress in 1928, the refuge is 64,895 acres big. It is a marvelous place for visits by wingless visitors of the human persuasion. The refuge is open to the public during the day, and if the visitor is diligent enough and has the time (and knowledge), he may be able to count some 200 species, about a third of which are nesting birds. If he would rather look than count, he would see, among others, such varieties as cormorants, gulls, terns, herons, egrets, swans, pelicans, teals, coots and grebes. Sometimes the scene resembles an open-air madhouse, with thousands of small bodies whirling about the skies, while other thousands jostle each other for swimming or standing space in the marshes. Even between migrations the refuge is where the action is, one of the few remaining places on the continent where tremendous concentrations of waterfowl can gather and nest.

The Scenic South

Mention the south of Utah, and Zion and Bryce Canyons come at once to mind. But these two very special places are not the sole repositories in the state of weird and wonderful vistas. The southlands are full of attractions that have not been included within national park boundaries. Some are in national monuments: Cedar Breaks, Natural Bridges, Hovenweep and Rainbow Bridge.

Up until the end of the second World War, only about 4,000 people were known to have made the trip to Rainbow Bridge, in spite of the fact that Theodore Roosevelt and others called it "the greatest natural wonder in the world." After driving to the end of the road and, from most accounts, a little beyond, the traveler still had a 16-mile packsaddle trip to endure — across five canyons, one of which was 2,000 feet deep. Because of its remoteness, Rainbow Bridge was not discovered by white men until 1909, when two men, seeking a legendary arch they had heard mentioned in Indian stories, were led to the site by a Paiute Indian guide.

The bridge lived up to the legends. Its Paiute name means "rainbow," and the Navajo name translates to something like "where the rock goes across." Of a brilliant salmon colored sandstone, the bridge arches high over Bridge Creek, 309 feet high, 42 feet thick and 33 feet wide at the top, spanning 278 feet. There is nothing to equal its grace and its monumental stature.

Today's visitor to Rainbow Bridge has a little easier time. Glen Canyon Dam has backed up the Colorado's waters to the point that boaters can get within a short walk of the majestic bridge; and in time of plentiful water, Bridge Creek — the Bridge's sculptor — flows beneath it.

The southwest is "Dixie" land, so-called because of its semi-tropical climate that brings rich return from farms in the Santa Clara and Virgin River valleys. But this is mainly desert country, high and dry; warm in winter and hot in summer. All the land around here, desert and valley, is around half-a-mile high. It's a nice place for a smallish canyon, not very well known, but special. This is Snow Canyon, a broad, dry gorge about three miles long near St. George, a town close to the Arizona border. The canyon floor is at the 2,000-foot level, full of volcanic rubble. There are cinder cones near the canyon's head, where the elevation is 3,500 feet. The source of the volcanism, though long dormant, is still present in the background. The Pine Valley Mountains, more than 10,300 feet high, are what remains of the gigantic caldera that in both ancient and recent geologic time spewed out the lava now scattered over the canyon floor. This little canyon (65,000 acres) is almost unknown, even by Utahans. But the mix of sandstone and lava rock there make it of more than passing interest. It's an honest-to-goodness canyon, too, with walls up to 750 feet high, done in red and buff Navajo sandstone. Considering the terrain and the climate, a wide variety of plant life has taken hold, in addition to the characteristic creosote and mesquite. Some of these are manzanita, pinon pine, hedgehog cactus, prickly pear, yucca, sagebrush, Mormon tea, desert holly, juniper, and saltbrush. Spring and fall bring a garden of flower species, adding to the diversity that makes Snow Canyon State Park worth the seeing.

A few miles north of Zion National Park is Cedar Breaks National Monument, another one of the fantastic and colorful phenomena of the high plateau country. A national monument, since 1933, it bears some affinities to Bryce Canyon 30 miles to the east. Cedar Breaks is more talented, even, than Bryce in the matter of color. And that's remarkable, because the other canyon's gorgeous colors contribute in a big way to its popularity. In both brilliance and range of tints, Cedar Breaks dazzles the eye. Its concentration into one huge area brings all that color within the frame of one glance. The brilliant red and gold, white and cream, deep rose, coral, orange, purple, green, and blue in many tonal variations make up a palette that no mortal painter ever possessed. The amphitheater of Cedar Breaks is far less extensive than Bryce, but both cut deep into the plateau — almost a half-mile in the case of Cedar Breaks. Cedar Breaks is much smaller, two miles from rim to rim of the abyss. Like Bryce it contains a multitude of forms in its giant basin, but on a more heroic scale. The filigree grotesques, labyrinthine passages, mazes, and grottoes of Bryce are absent. Here the chasm steps down in terraces, and as the visitor gazes into the bowl from a place on the rim, he cannot fail to be amazed at the scope and perfection of the sandstone shapes that line the floor and walls of the canyon. Like Bryce, it has the aura of a city of stone, a fantasy city that once housed living creatures. Its towers, pinnacles, and walls seem to be waiting for the return of residents temporarily detained somewhere else. But there's something wrong with that fantasy: Cedar Breaks was "breaking" long before *homo sapiens* were ever thought of.

Roads in this forbidding land are an impossibility. The only human visitor with assured entry is the foot traveler. In places such as the Pariah's Buckskin Gulch, man is an alien form of life. These deep, tight canyons seem to have been designed to keep him out; points of access and egress are very few. Their walls are vertical cliffs that drop down to sandy, gravelly beds where wheels would be an absurdity and footing, even, is difficult. To add to the thrill, there are areas of quicksand. To add further to the thrill, flash floods come thundering down the canyon during summer storms. But the possibility of being washed into the next county is of little moment to the canyon freak, who glories in picking his way along a rocky, oozy streambed, shut off from the world by sinuous rock cliffs that stretch far into the sky above him.

Coyote Gulch is one of the bigger side canyons in the Escalante system. It is an especially beautiful example of the unique wilderness experience that can be found in these sinuous corridors of stone. In the depths of Coyote's chasm is a different world from the harsh desert regime that rules the canyon rims. The walls that twist and wander along the stream course provide living environments not possible in the open desert high above. In certain magic corners of the canyon, the opposite walls play off the sunlight against each other at the right time of day. The sun's glare, reflected from one wall into an alcove across the canyon, creates a strange radiance in that niche that is almost palpable.

Over the river (Colorado) and past the lake (Powell) is southeastern Utah. In this corner of the state, the San Juan River's "gooseneck" canyons are one of nature's great mystifications. West of the town of Bluff, the wildly meandering river has chewed a series of closely spaced canyons like rounded-off zig-zags. These are indeed called the Goosenecks, where the river makes long loops covering about six miles to travel only one. About five airline miles from where the San Juan joins the Colorado is the greatest bend of all, called, appropriately, the Great Bend. Here the river makes a nine-mile loop and ends up half a mile from its starting point. The erratic course of the river continues beyond even this point: the San Juan travels 34 miles to cover the five straight-line miles to the Colorado River.

North of the river town of Bluff and west of Blanding is Natural Bridges National Monument, another area of Utah where the plateau has eroded into fantastic formations. It was carved primarily by rain water and ancestral San Juan River water courses. The rain water rode the high, tilted plateau on its way to the sea, creating first cracks, then canyons to depths of 2,500 feet in some places. The wandering arms of the river cut deep scallops in these canyons where the stream looped around and back upon itself. Soft, underlying rock in the necks of these loops was undermined and eventually washed out by the strong currents beating against them. Where the upper rock layers were harder, bridges of rock were left. Three splendid examples of these rock spans are found in canyons of the national monument. The oldest is believed to be Owachomo — about 10 million years. The bridge is located at the monument's southern boundary. Its 10-foot-thick span, salmon pink, crosses 200-foot Armstrong Canyon at a height of 108 feet.

Three miles farther south in the canyon is Kachina Bridge, more substantial and darker red than the other two bridges. It is 107 feet thick and more, with a 186-foot span towering to 205 feet above the canyon. Not far from Kachina is lower White Canyon, and some three-and-a-half miles up this gorge is the finest of the three structures — Simpapu Bridge. It has been called noble and symmetrical, and that it surely is. It is also big. The span is 261 feet high, arching 222 feet over the canyon.

Hovenweep National Monument occupies a small area north of the San Juan River on either side of the Utah-Colorado border. The preserve was established in 1923 to protect the remains of something man-made, measured in merely thousands of years. These are the ruins of prehistoric Indian civilization, contained in four separate groups of buildings set in various of these remote canyons of southeast Utah and southwest Colorado.

Ruin Canyon, on the Utah side, contains most of the important buildings in Hovenweep. A steep-walled gorge as much as 500 feet deep, it begins with an abrupt drop from a mesa a few miles north of the San Juan River. Up on the mesa wall are the Pueblo ruins. The best preserved dwellings are in Ruin Canyon and Square Tower Canyon, which splits off from Ruin. The remarkable condition of Hovenweep's Pueblo treasures is a testimonial to their sheltered location and to southern Utah's high, dry plateau country. This strangely paradoxical land, with its feeling of fragile timelessness, may have bestowed a part of its own immortal spirit on one of the passing works of man.

Utah

State Capital: *Salt Lake City*

State Flower: *Sego Lily*

State Nickname: *Beehive State*

State Bird: *Seagull*

State Motto: *Industry*

State Tree: *Blue Spruce*

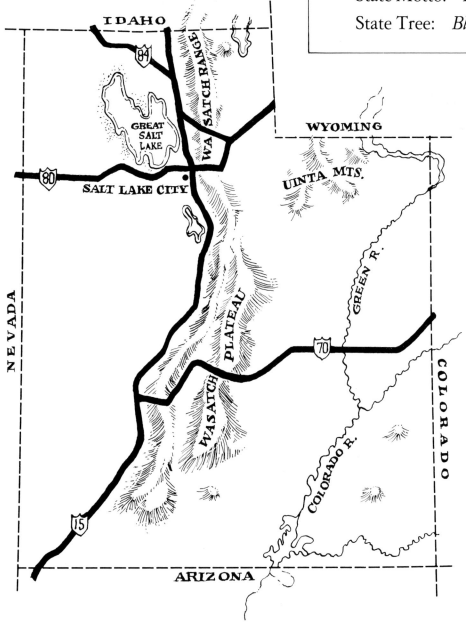